Florence Nightingale

Mother of Modern Nursing

by Carol Alexander

Content Consultant

Nanci R. Vargus, Ed.D.
Professor Emeritus, University of Indianapolis

Reading Consultant

Jeanne M. Clidas, Ph.D.
Reading Specialist

Children's Press®
An Imprint of Scholastic Inc.

Library of Congress Cataloging-in-Publication Data
Alexander, Carol, 1955-
  Florence Nightingale / by Carol Alexander ; poem by Jodie Shepherd.
    pages cm. -- (Rookie biographies)
  Includes index.
  ISBN 978-0-531-21412-1 (library binding) -- ISBN 978-0-531-21425-1 (pbk.)
  1. Nightingale, Florence, 1820-1910--Juvenile literature. 2. Nurses--England--
Biography--Juvenile literature. I. Shepherd, Jodie. II. Title.
  RT37.N5A456 2015
  610.73--dc23   2015017319

Produced by Spooky Cheetah Press
Poem by Jodie Shepherd
Design by Keith Plechaty

© 2016 by Scholastic Inc.

Printed in China 62

SCHOLASTIC, CHILDREN'S PRESS, ROOKIE BIOGRAPHIES®, and associated logos
are trademarks and/or registered trademarks of Scholastic Inc.

1 2 3 4 5 6 7 8 9 10 R 25 24 23 22 21 20 19 18 17 16

Photographs ©: cover: Bettmann/Corbis Images; 3 top left: Stockbyte/Thinkstock;
3 top right: hxdbzxy/Shutterstock, Inc.; 3 bottom: catwalker/Shutterstock, Inc.; 4:
Photos.com/Thinkstock; 8: Chris Foard; 11: SuperStock/Getty Images; 12: Interfoto/
Alamy Images; 16: English School/Getty Images; 19: Stapleton Collection/Corbis
Images; 20: Popperfoto/Getty Images; 23: Wellcome Library, London; 24 top:
lantapix/iStockphoto; 24 center: Iriana Shiyan/Shutterstock, Inc.; 24 bottom:
Imagesbybarbara/iStockphoto; 27: Mary Evans Picture Library/Alamy Images; 28:
david Riley/Alamy Images; 30 top left: Photos.com/Thinkstock; 30 top right: david
Riley/Alamy Images; 31 top: SuperStock/Getty Images; 31 center top: Corepics VOF/
Shutterstock, Inc.; 31 center bottom: hxdbzxy/Shutterstock, Inc.; 31 bottom: Mary
Evans Picture Library/Alamy Images.

Maps by XNR Productions, Inc.

Table of Contents

Meet Florence Nightingale

Imagine if you went to the hospital and it was dirty. Or if your doctor did not wash her hands! That is what life was like in the 1800s. People did not know how to stop **germs** from going from one person to another.

Florence Nightingale was a nurse. She helped make hospitals cleaner. She taught doctors and nurses how to keep clean. Her hard work saved many lives.

Nightingale was born on May 12, 1820, in Italy. Her family moved to England when Florence was a baby. She grew up in a huge house with servants and fancy clothes. Her family was very rich.

Many of Florence's neighbors were poor. She helped them whenever she could. She often took care of them when they got sick.

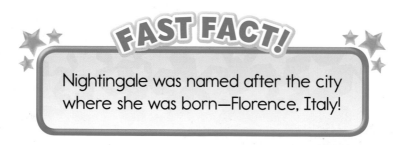

FAST FACT!

Nightingale was named after the city where she was born—Florence, Italy!

MAP KEY

Italy

● Town where Florence Nightingale was born

■ Town where Florence Nightingale grew up

North Sea

England

Hampshire

Italy

Florence

Area enlarged

Mediterranean Sea

7

Most rich girls like Florence did not go to school. But she wanted to learn. She wanted to learn math. She wanted to learn to speak different languages. She wanted to become a nurse.

This is a photo of Florence's childhood home in England.

Florence's parents did not want her to be a nurse. Hospitals were dirty places! The sick people who went there were usually poor. Young ladies like Florence were supposed to get married and raise a family.

But Florence was **determined.** She wanted to be a nurse no matter what.

Florence worked hard in school. She had big dreams.

At last, Florence talked her parents into sending her to nursing school. In 1851, she studied nursing in Germany. She was there for three months. She worked hard.

When she got back home, Florence was a nurse! She went to work in a hospital in London, England. She loved helping other people.

Florence studied at one of the first training centers for nursing.

13

War!

In 1853, a war broke out. There was fighting in the country of Turkey. Many soldiers were getting hurt. The hospital needed nurses.

The English government asked Nightingale to help. She went to Turkey to take care of the soldiers. She took 38 other nurses with her.

Nightingale Goes from England to Turkey

MAP KEY

Turkey

Florence Nightingale's journey to Turkey

● Hospital where Florence Nightingale worked

England

Black Sea

Scutari hospital

Turkey

Mediterranean Sea

Area enlarged

15

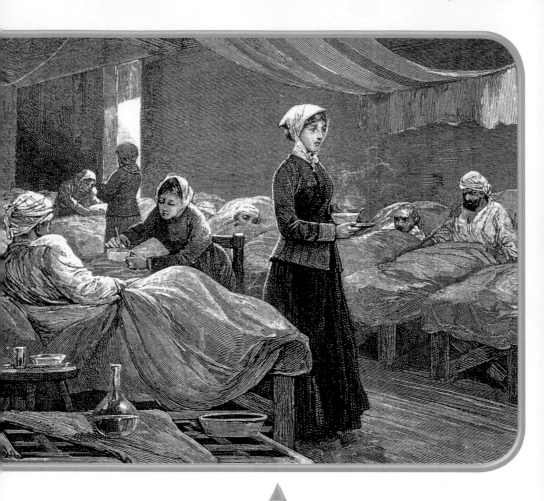

This is the hospital in Turkey where Nightingale worked.

At the hospital, **hygiene** was poor. That means it was very dirty. There were not even enough beds or bandages for the soldiers. They were dying from all the germs that were in the hospital.

Nightingale made sure the hospital was scrubbed from top to bottom. She wrote reports and letters asking for supplies. She paid for some things herself.

The Lady with the Lamp

Nightingale and her nurses worked day and night. In the evenings, Nightingale carried a lamp. The hospital did not have electric lights. She need the lamp to see.

The soldiers called her "the Lady with the Lamp." She made sure they had medicine, food, and clean blankets. The soldiers were very grateful.

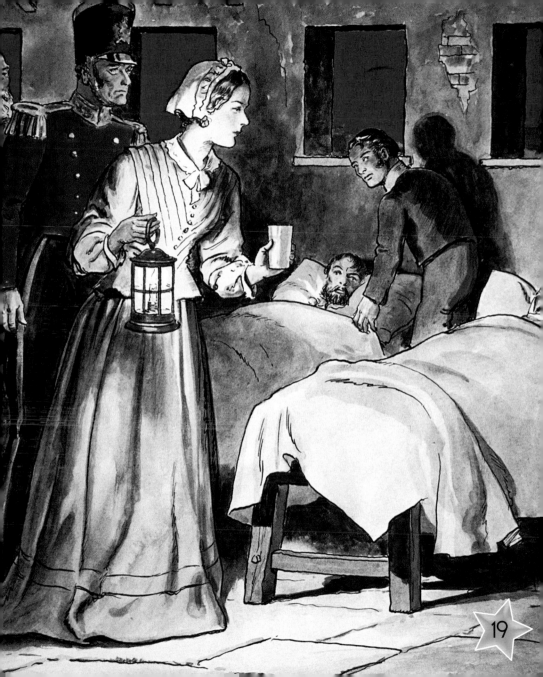

For many months, Nightingale nursed the soldiers. She became very ill, but she would not stop working. She was determined to help the men in her care. She would not give up.

Nightingale worked where the battles were fought.

Helping at Home

After the war, many people back home asked Nightingale for help. The government asked her how to make hospitals better.

Nightingale was happy to share what she knew. She wrote books and reports. Her most famous book was *Notes on Nursing*. In the book, Nightingale explained how to make hospitals better.

NOTES ON NURSING:

WHAT IT IS, AND WHAT IT IS NOT.

BY

FLORENCE NIGHTINGALE.

This is the title page from one of Nightingale's books.

LONDON:

HARRISON, 59, PALL MALL,

BOOKSELLER TO THE QUEEN.

In her book, Nightingale explained the job of a nurse. Hospital workers had to keep patients' rooms clean. It was important that sick people got lots of fresh air and sunlight. All nurses had to scrub their hands with soap and clean water. They had to serve plain, healthy meals to the patients.

In 1860, Nightingale started a school for nurses. She **trained** the nurses. She taught them to make hospitals clean and safe.

Nightingale decided one school for nurses was not enough. She started more schools in other countries, too!

Nurses from Nightingale's schools went to work in hospitals around the world.

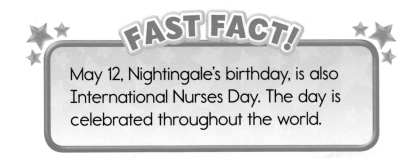

FAST FACT!

May 12, Nightingale's birthday, is also International Nurses Day. The day is celebrated throughout the world.

Nightingale (center) is shown with some of her students.

Timeline of Florence Nightingale's Life

1821
moves to England

1854
goes to Turkey

1820
born in Florence, Italy

1851
studies nursing in Germany

Florence Nightingale lived to be 90 years old. She showed many people how to become nurses. She helped change hospitals and health care around the world. She saved the lives of many people. And she improved the lives of many more!

1860
founds the Florence Nightingale Training School for nurses; publishes *Notes on Nursing*

1910
dies on August 13

A Poem About Florence Nightingale

When Florence Nightingale became a nurse,

hospitals could not have been much worse.

She cleaned things up, let in the sun—

better health for everyone!

You Can Make a Difference

- Make cards for family members who are feeling sick. That will cheer them up!

- Always be willing to lend a hand. You might help a neighbor shovel snow or help your parent carry groceries.

Glossary

determined (dih-TUR-mind): having made a firm decision to do something

germs (JURMZ): tiny living things that cause sickness

hygiene (HYE-jeen): what people do to stay healthy and keep clean

trained (TRAYND): taught people how to do something

Index

Facts for Now

Visit this Scholastic Web site for more information on Florence Nightingale:
www.factsfornow.scholastic.com
Enter the keywords **Florence Nightingale**

About the Author

Carol Alexander has written both fiction and nonfiction for children and young adults. Her poetry appears in many magazines and books. Alexander has taught in colleges around the New York City area and now works in publishing. She lives in New York with her family and pets.